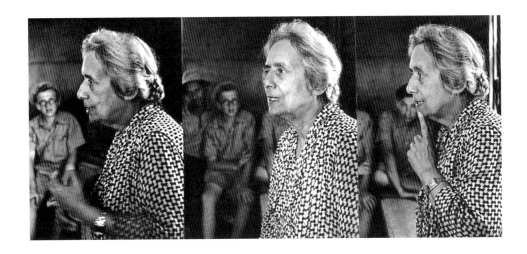

To my wife Pia, one of the 13,000

Designed by Ora Yafeh

Gidal, Nachum Tim, 1909 - 1996
Henrietta Szold : The Saga of an American Woman / Nachum T. Gidal.
p.   cm.
ISBN 965-229-162-5
1. Szold, Henrietta, 1860-1945.
2. Zionists--United States--Biography.
3. Jewish Agency for Israel. Youth Aliyah Dept.-Pictorial works.
4. Szold, Henrietta, 1860-1945–Portraits.

I. Title.
DS151.S9G53   1996
320.5'4'095694092–dc20
II.   96-34551
         CIP

Edition 9 8 7 6 5 4 3 2 1

Gefen Publishing House Ltd.   Gefen Books
POB 36004, Jerusalem   12 New St., Hewlett
91360 Israel   NY, U.S.A. 11557

Photographs on pages: 55, 56 bottom, 58, 59, 60, 61, 62,
 64, 66, 67 are by Sonia Epstein - © Nachum T. Gidal

Printed in Israel

Send for our free catalogue

HENRIETTA SZOLD

A DOCUMENTATION IN PHOTOS AND TEXT

NACHUM TIM GIDAL

gefen
publishing house בית הוצאה לאור

In memory of Henrietta Szold,
I dedicate this book to the women of
Hadassah, who contributed, with
passion, so much to the saving of
children and betterment of humankind.

NACHUM TIM GIDAL

Henrietta Szold on a tour of Kibbutzim in the Galilee

CONTENTS

"I expect to pass through this world but once.

Any good thing, therefore, that I can do, or

Any kindness that I can show to any fellow-creature

Let me do it now.

Let me not defer or neglect it.

For I shall not pass this way again."

These lines from the poem *The Cry of the Children*
by Elizabeth Barrett Browning, were found in a drawer of
her desk after Henrietta Szold's death.

I REMEMBER...

Zionist Congress in Lucerne, 1935. Henrietta Szold explains the Youth Aliyah Organization. It is her 75th birthday

A small, fragile looking lady crossed to the speaker's rostrum. She spoke clearly and simply. She told her audience of the work on the great project, of the many difficulties, of the lack of money for the countless essential preparations. But she was full of optimism too.

"Were I not close to seventy-five, I would dare to make promises... When I think how much dignity our German victims have displayed, and that I was privileged to help to some extent, I must say in all modesty, 'The dear God has dealt well with me'."

Who was this woman who, Biblical in years, dared to undertake the task of saving Jewish children from Jew-killing Germany, transplanting them to the Land of Israel, there to educate them to become first-class citizens.

During the summer of 1932, I travelled through Poland, together with two friends. All over that country we found like-minded friends of the Zionist movements. They had been waiting for years for permission to immigrate to Palestine, to the Land of Israel. The British mandatory authorities granted entry permits only to very few immigrants from Eastern Europe. More than 50,000 young Zionists, trained in agriculture as well as many crafts, were waiting desperately, kicking their heels, joining the outlawed Communist Party in their frustration.

At that time, Hanoch R., one of my two travel companions, told me of a social worker in Berlin, Recha Freier. She planned to bring fourteen and fifteen-year-old children to Palestine. But it seemed impossible to finance such a huge project and carry it through. "One day her plan will be realized," Hanoch said, "Recha Freier is convinced of that, although she is not a great organizer. Maybe, such an idea could be put into effect here in Poland too, because Palestinian immigration law does not apply to children of this age."

I knew Recha Freier. She had introduced me to a Zionist Youth Group, which I had joined in Munich at the age of ten. Her father had been our Hebrew teacher, teaching me at home.

In the year after our journey to Poland, the anti-Semites came to power in Germany.

In the fall of the year 1933, an elderly lady arrived in Berlin from Palestine. She had come to bring Recha Freier's project to fruition, because Recha wasn't sufficiently experienced to organize it. This elderly lady was an American by birth, but she spoke German and Hebrew fluently. Her name was Henrietta Szold. At 73, after twenty-three years of social work in Jewish Palestine, she had that same spring made a final tour of the country before packing her bags to spend the rest of her days with her family in Baltimore, USA. But when the anti-Semites came to power, she unpacked her bags again.

"There is no hope," she wrote at that time, "as many fondly believe, that the Nazi terror is, or can be made, a passing phenomenon. Hitler and his hordes have come to bide a while in this torn, agitated world of ours. It will be cause for gratitude if they do not ignite another world war."

In Berlin, Henrietta Szold achieved cooperation between different organizations engaged in the work of preparing children for emigration to Israel. She demanded that the boys and girls should be no younger than fifteen and no older than seventeen, and should be selected on the basis of health and educational standards, not party affiliation. She stipulated that no group should come to Palestine before the project was firmly established financially and before sufficient suitable dormitories and classrooms for the children were built in the settlements.

The first group of forty-three boys and girls, under the guidance of Hanoch R., arrived in Haifa in February 1934. There, Henrietta Szold was waiting for them and accompanied them to their new home in the collective settlement 'En Harod in the Jezreel Valley. Miss Szold described the reception

With the gardener of Ashdot Ya'aqov

they received there as being "like a religious poem." I saw this group in spring 1935, at work and in the classrooms.

Henrietta Szold I met for the first time at the Zionist Congress held in August of that year in Lucerne, Switzerland. The building was hung with black flags, a token of shocked mourning and protest against the anti-Jewish terror in Germany. Zionist delegates from many countries discussed plans for saving German Jews.

Professor Chaim Weizmann, for many years the leader of the Zionist Movement, and later the first President of the State of Israel, spoke. He was holding a bouquet of roses in his hands: "I intended to present these flowers as a farewell gift and as a token of the gratitude of our people to a woman who will be seventy-five this year - to my friend Henrietta Szold. It was really meant to be a farewell gift. But now I want to thank her, who loves flowers so much, for a new task, which she has undertaken: this task is to save our children, as many as possible. Henrietta Szold, there is work for you in Zion!"

CHILDHOOD AND YOUTH

Henrietta Szold's father, Benjamin, as a student at the Breslau Rabbinical Seminary, 1856

Her father, Benjamin Szold, son of a Jewish farmer in Hungary, concluded his studies as a rabbi at a
very young age. He studied for the rabbinate at the famous Rabbinical Seminary in Breslau, Germany. A
brilliant scholar and preacher, he maintained that the moral principles of the Jewish faith must be
fulfilled in every situation of life.   Faith and daily life were for him an indissoluble whole: the one had to
be manifested constantly in the other.

Abraham Lincoln.

In 1859, the twenty-seven year old Dr. Benjamin Szold was appointed
to the post of rabbi in Baltimore, Maryland. Here Henrietta was born
on December 21, 1860, the first of eight daughters.

Her most vivid childhood memories were of the Civil War for the
liberation of the Negro slaves - and the assassination of President
Lincoln. Abraham Lincoln was the idol of the Szold family.

One day, a member of the family lifted her on his shoulders and
carried her solemnly across to the window, "Look! You will see them
now, bearing Abraham Lincoln to his grave."

She once told me that this experience determined the course of her
life to a great degree.

Many inhabitants of Baltimore were of German origin. In those days,
there were two German newspapers in town, a German theatre and

Abraham Lincoln's funeral procession passes through Baltimore

German schools. Dr. Szold preached in German to his congregation of immigrants from Germany, Austria, Hungary, Bohemia. So did the Catholic and Protestant priests and ministers in their churches. The neighbors spoke German dialects, and Henrietta spoke a mixture of Bavarian and Swabian, before she started to learn English in the private school, which her father had started in the basement of the synagogue. "But my real education I received at the family table, where we would all gather for hours, talking about the problems of the day. The problems of the world were freely discussed, and every event of public life was related to the teachings of Judaism, to anecdotes from Jewish literature and Jewish popular humor. There was nothing dry or solemn about these discussions. Our laughter could often be heard in the street below."

At sixteen, Henrietta finished her education at the Girls' High School as the best of 48 pupils, only to return there immediately for fifteen years, to teach German, French, Algebra and Botany. In addition, she taught Religion and Jewish History on Saturdays and Sundays, and continued her studies in Hebrew, the Bible and the Talmud with her father.

She began to contribute regularly to various periodicals, progressive articles on contemporary events and educational questions. She also made outspoken attacks against religious hypocrisy and political and social oppression, no matter by whom: be it an intolerant rabbi, the Tsar of Russia, or a cowardly anti-Semite. In those days, she recognized the problem of the Jew as one of "living amongst a Christian majority without damage to one's soul." As a consequence, it was above all the training of educators with which she concerned herself.

"Not knowledge, but the capacity to *acquire* knowledge, is power," the twenty-seven year old Henrietta Szold proclaimed in a lecture to teachers, "The true educator is a psychologist, who above all things will most assiduously acquaint himself or herself with the workings of the child's mind... It is the living, the organic, the concrete... that in life which throbs and pulsates like its own quickening blood, which attracts the child. In everything the child studies it must be shown growth - which is life."

CAREER AND CALLING

HAMBURG   An Bord des Auswandererdampfers

Jewish immigrants on board ship to U.S.A. (about 1905)

In 1882, with the blessing of the Russian Orthodox Church, and supported by most of the Russian aristocracy, the Tsar proclaimed the notorious May Laws. In its cynical brutality, government policy was symptomatic of the rottenness and decadence of Russian society and of the Russian state in general: a third of the Jewish population was to be forced to accept the Christian faith, one third was to be forced to emigrate, one third was to be killed. This program was introduced by a pogrom initiated by the government in all countries under Russian domination. For once, the shocked conscience of the world was roused to protest, and further massacres were prevented for the time being. But measures to starve the Jews through economic strangulation were enforced. From these measures they never again recovered.

There was no sign of the anticipated mass conversion to Christianity, for Judaism as a spiritual and religious force remained unshaken. But hundreds of thousands emigrated, mostly to America, the land of liberty. Many came to Baltimore; poverty-stricken, undernourished, ignorant of the language, insecure.

Many of them found their way to Rabbi Szold's house. For nights on end, the émigrés would sit around the table, which was always set in readiness for new guests. During these nights, Henrietta Szold came to understand and appreciate the spiritual force of the Enlightenment, which was alive especially in the young. They were no longer content with the suffering of the Jewish people made into a religious credo, but were yearning for fulfillment in *this* world and in *this* age.

Henrietta Szold sought practical help. First, the path had to be smoothed for immigrants in their new homeland. She rented a room. Together with voluntary helpers, she cleaned and furnished it, and started an evening school. Thirty pupils came on the first evening, old people and youngsters. By the light of an oil lamp, she began teaching them the new language, the history of America, its laws, and the principles of its democratic constitution. After a few months, the number had swelled to five hundred. In addition to teaching, she was committed to looking for other teachers, for rooms, for books, and for the essential financial means. These, of course, were always inadequate - American Jewry as such was poor at the time, rich Jews were still rare exceptions. Henrietta Szold set up a daily schedule to which she adhered, as a minimum program, to the end of her life: every morning from six until eight o'clock she worked at her correspondence. Then came her main job until four in the afternoon. After that, until eleven at night, the second, unpaid job: her vocation of working for social improvements. In those years, it was the organizing of evening schools for new immigrants.

Over five thousand students passed through this evening school in the course of the years in Baltimore. Soon after, evening schools, modelled after hers, were established in all the larger cities. To this day, they remain the original pattern for one of the great institutions in America, in which wave upon wave of immigrants were, and still are, educated as American citizens. Through them, they assimilate the cultural life of the new country and learn its language. This gives them the opportunity to take up the challenge of economic life.

Many years later, when Fiorello H. La Guardia, the Mayor of New York, named Henrietta Szold an Honorary Citizen of the city, he said in his speech: "Maybe I would not be here today, in 1936, if you had not started your work of educating the immigrant in 1882. I am the son of poor Italian immigrants. What I learned, I owe to the evening schools for immigrants."

Henrietta Szold's Russian students rewarded their teacher with the experience of a newly reawakened Judaism, of Zionism. "I was prepared for Zionism , because my father's attitude was that Judaism is a way of life, not only a faith or a creed. And the Russian immigrants gave me the vision of a living future for my people... I became converted to Zionism the very moment I realized that it supplied my bruised, torn, and bloody nation, my distracted nation, with an ideal - an ideal that is balm to the self-inflicted wounds and to the wounds inflicted by others."

In 1893, together with her friends, she founded the first Zionist association in Baltimore. That same year, she gave up her job as a teacher and, probably one of the most learned women in America, became the literary secretary of the Jewish Publication Society in Philadelphia. She gave new life to this non-profit making publishing enterprise. She translated some twenty works. She discovered authors, helped them in their writing, edited the manuscripts, supervised the printing, organized the sales and the enlisting of new subscribers. For twenty-three years, up to 1916, this was her main job.

In the meantime, her sisters had married. Henrietta Szold, surrounded in her youth by many admirers, charming, womanly, but outside the sphere of her work overly shy, had not married. She did not allow herself time for any private life. "But I would exchange everything for one child of my own," she once admitted.

* * *

In 1903, following the death of her father, she moved with her mother to New York. She continued to direct the Jewish Publication Society from there, also studying at the Jewish Theological Seminary and undertaking lecture tours. It was during this period that she collaborated with Louis Ginzberg on his *Legends of the Jews*, and translated this work, which in the meantime has become a classic, into English. It was, in every sense of the word her labor of love.

She also found here the great love of her life - but it did not lead to marriage. The storm shook her all the more strongly since it came so late. It ended in a severe nervous illness, from which she recovered very slowly. Afterwards, accompanied by her mother, she went on a journey to Europe and to Palestine, the Land of Israel.

1909 JOURNEY TO PALESTINE

Jerusalem. In the foreground, the Western Wall of Herod's Temple

At first in England, and then in France and Italy, Henrietta Szold experienced deep emotions when she saw works of art she had previously known merely through reproductions. She was moved by the humanity of Rembrandt, the elegiac spirituality in Botticelli's quest for beauty, the dramatic realism of Velasquez. But the theatrical splendor of Rubens and Veronese - or was it their ostensible sensuality - not only left her cold, but went against her grain.

Jaffa Gate in 1909, with travelling coach such as was used by Henrietta Szold and her mother

In the cathedrals and in their works of religious art, in the cult of the Madonna and in the choral music of the church, she saw the supreme expression of dedication to an ideal. In St. Mark's in Venice, she witnessed High Mass, celebrated in overwhelming magnificence as the symbol of an invisible power, and she thought, almost despairingly, of her own "poor people, knocking at the door of humanity and begging only for the right to live."

The two Szolds continued their journey. Henrietta's mother was seventy years old, Henrietta was forty-nine. They travelled by way of Constantinople, Alexandria, Beirut and Damascus. From there, travelling by horse-drawn cart, they went to Jerusalem.

It was a city for pilgrims, but it was not much of a living city at that time. Most of the 14,000 inhabitants lived in tumbledown stone huts. The two women encountered epidemics, trachoma and undernourishment. The average daily income of a worker was twenty cents, an income which could only be increased by begging.

When Henrietta Szold looked across to the "Wailing Wall" as the Christians called it, and to the noble beauty of the Temple square behind it, which once carried the Temple of Solomon on its platform, her spirit rebelled against the depressed state the Holy City had fallen into, and she expressed her feelings in many letters home.

She stayed in Jerusalem with her mother for twelve days. Afterwards, they moved on to Jaffa, Haifa, Tiberias, and to the Jewish agricultural settlements. There, the settlers barely managed to subsist. They were weakened by dysentery and malaria. Most were without any medical care whatsoever, but they endured in the knowledge of being pioneers, building up their land. "I learned to love its grayness, its stones, its terraces, its varied richness. It is the only possible refuge for our people. If we fail, I see no hope for our fragments," she wrote home.

Henrietta wrote long reports to her Zionist group back in America, and wondered how their common love for Zion could be put to a more practical use. "When she wondered, she pondered, when she pondered, she looked for practical solutions," a friend said of her. And she was a stiff-necked and powerful organizer with an imperturbable will, which would not and could not be sidetracked, once she had made up her strong mind. Many officials and politicians were to encounter this strong will in later years, from Zionist Organization officials to Ben Gurion. She never ceded a point when it went against her better knowledge. This is perhaps the reason why her two great creations, Hadassah and Youth Aliyah, almost without exception, never bogged down in the maze of bureaucratic red tape in which Jewish organizations in Palestine excelled even then.

In Jaffa, mother and daughter were shocked by the sight of many children who had trachoma and whose eyes were infested with flies. But visiting a Jewish girls' school they found not a single case of trachoma. "How is it that all these children are perfectly healthy, while outside, there are children in such awful conditions?" they asked the principal of the school. He replied: "That is simple; we have a physician who visits us twice a week, and a nurse who comes daily. They take care of the eyes!" As they emerged, her mother said: "That is what your group ought to do. What is the use of reading papers and arranging festivals? *You should do practical work in Palestine.*"

"HEALING MY PEOPLE..."

Travelling in Judea, ca. 1909

Back in America, Henrietta Szold, together with fourteen like-minded women, made the necessary preparations. She founded an all-American organization named HADASSAH, the Hebrew name of the Persian Jewish Queen Esther. The aim of this Zionist women's organization was expressed in the words of the prophet Jeremiah, which the founders chose as the motto for their work:

"Behold the voice of the cry of my people...
Is there no balm in Gilead?
Is there no physician there?
Why then is not the healing of my people accomplished?"
(8.22)

Henrietta Szold began organizing Hadassah to include the necessary financing of relief work and its practical implementation in Palestine. The following year, it was already possible to send the first two nurses there.

At the outbreak of the First World War in 1914, most of the doctors in Palestine were deported as enemy Russians by the Turks. Epidemics and starvation were rife. Henrietta Szold and her co-workers increased their efforts and secured the collaboration of other organizations.

At the end of the war, when it was again possible at last to enter the country, a medical expedition, consisting of twenty doctors, twenty nurses and five technical assistants, left New York for Palestine. Although some of the doctors and nurses had never been on a horse before, nevertheless, on the day of their landing, they began to ride on horseback. Almost without stopping, they rode for twenty-six hours all the way to Tiberias. The plague had broken out there. Tiberias had no doctor, no drugs. Three quarters of the Jewish and Arab population were sick with cholera at home or lying in the streets.

That was the start of the "Medical Expedition" which, under the direction of Henrietta Szold, was to develop, in the course of long and difficult years, into the Health System of Jewish Palestine, and later of Israel. Today, over three hundred thousand women are active members of this Hadassah Organization. Hospitals, hygiene, the training of nurses, institutes for medical research are the results of their work.

At the beginning of 1920, Henrietta Szold came to Palestine to take over the local direction of the "Medical Expedition", which had now run into financial and organizational difficulties. Before she left America, she brought her work as director of the Zionist Education Department to an end. "I shall leave the office, start to think about my clothes, pack and make my will, for I plan a two-year stay in Palestine", she wrote to a friend.

She remained in Palestine, with short interruptions, for nearly twenty-five years, to the end of her life. "There's work in Zion which has to be done," she reported soon after her arrival. She always liked to sprinkle her often sober day-to-day work with some spiritual pronouncement and vice versa.

Her first task was to introduce order into the chaotic health system of the country, perpetually struggling for the necessary minimum budget.

Again and again, the British Government idly watched the attacks against Jewish settlements in which hundreds of Jews were killed. Again and again, defenders of such settlements were sentenced to long terms of imprisonment, if found in possession of weapons for self-defense. The majority of British administrative officials were intolerant or openly hostile to Jewish construction. The minority was powerless, especially as Sir Herbert Samuel, the first British High Commissioner, a British Jew, often leaned over backwards to appease the Arabs. The Jews, unlike the populations of most British Colonies and mandated countries, were not prepared to let themselves be treated as subservient "natives". Henrietta Szold became indignant and shocked at the attitude of most of the British here, for she had come to know them at home, in their own country, as humane and fair. She expressed her indignation in strong terms. Moreover, she also had to fight against the narrowness of the political party spirit and the lack of understanding of her own people in her attempts to build up a *non-party* educational system.

Before long, she was directing the whole Jewish health service. She also temporarily took over the education system, and finally, she organized the Social Services.

In the meantime, her working day had grown to sixteen hours: "My day extends from 4:30 in the morning until midnight and I am kept busy all hours."

In answer to the question, how she was able to cope with such an extraordinarily long working day in the hot and exhausting Palestine climate, she once answered: "There are two reasons: one, I keep the Sabbath; and two, my cast iron stomach."

* * *

In the spring of 1933, Henrietta Szold at last decided to retire into private life. She was seventy-four. But then, the barbarians came to power in Germany. Henrietta Szold was asked to help. There was no one like herself, capable of integrating young people into Israel.

Henrietta Szold accepted the task. She transformed Recha Freier's idea into workable practice. She organized Youth Aliyah, the "Ascent" of Youth to the Land of Israel.

THE RESCUE

Top: First Youth Aliyah group arrives from Germany, 1934
Bottom: The first Youth Aliyah group, 'En Harod, 1934

More than one million children were murdered during the years of the German massacres. During the last twelve years of her life, from those destined to be killed, Henrietta Szold saved approximately thirteen thousand. Through 1996, Youth Aliyah institutions have brought 300,000 youth to Israel.

Once in Israel, these children were not only provided with food and shelter, they were also educated and trained for two years in rural settlements. In the realization of this task, Henrietta Szold was assisted by a group of associates who carried on the work after her death, bringing children to Israel from the concentration camps of Europe, from Buchenwald, Bergen Belsen, from Mauthausen and Auschwitz. About fifty thousand followed from Poland and Hungary, from Bulgaria and Turkey, from Egypt, Yemen and Iraq. By 1960, the number of children saved had risen to one hundred thousand. When this kind of immigration came to an end, Youth Aliyah undertook a new task: teachers, welfare workers and instructors were trained in special seminaries. Many of them had been Youth Aliyah children themselves a few years before.

The funds necessary for this project came, and still are, mainly provided by the women of the Hadassah organization in America, from W.I.Z.O. (Women's International Zionist Organization) in Canada, England, Australia, and from similar bodies in England and South Africa, in Australia, in Switzerland and in Israel itself. All donations are anonymous, no child knows the name of individual benefactors, just as no donor knows which individual child has been saved or educated by his or her contribution. "Whoever saves a single life saves humanity." This saying of the Jewish tradition remained the maxim of the enterprise and the satisfaction of all those who helped in this work.

Henrietta Szold said: "My present life, intimately connected with the Jewry preparing to be the rebuilders of a nation, is full and rich..."

The first groups from Germany arrived in the spring of 1934. They were well-prepared and equipped. This was soon to change, with the increasing threat to the lives of German Jews.

After the third and last visit to Berlin in 1937, she reported: "The Jews in Germany are living corpses. They are capable of only one emotion - fear. They are furtive, listless, scared. Those over forty-five or fifty have resigned themselves to their fate - they will rot in Germany. Their one cry is: *Save the young!*"

It became increasingly difficult to obtain immigration certificates for Palestine. Applications for a single permit often involved many months of negotiations, and in each case a guarantee of full financial support for a two-year stay had to be provided. "When I have to deal with the delays and obstacles which the British government delights in interposing, I rage and despair."

From 1934 up to the outbreak of the Second World War, some five thousand children from Germany, Austria, Poland and Czechoslovakia were brought to Palestine by Youth Aliyah.

Henrietta Szold visits one of the first Youth Aliyah groups, winter 1934/5

JERUSALEM

Top: The Youth Aliyah office in a private house in Jerusalem
Bottom: At home with her secretary Emma Ehrlich

Henrietta Szold loved Jerusalem, where she spent nearly twenty-five years of her life.

In the course of these years, the new suburbs of Jerusalem transformed it from a squalid town into a modern city with a vital population. Modern residential districts developed, with gardens, avenues, well-built stone houses, schools, hospitals and a university.

The return of the Jews to their own land was symbolized for Henrietta Szold in both the development of the agricultural settlements and in the reconstruction of the Holy City, "I believe firmly that our truly great achievements have been possible only because we built on the foundation of sentiment, and Zionist sentiment is embodied now and forever in Jerusalem. Jerusalem is testimony and promise, the glory of the past and the greater spiritual glory of the future."

This city became the center of her work for the children.

She lived in Rehavia, a modern residential quarter, only a few hundred yards away from the little house in Ibn Gabirol Road, which housed the Youth Aliyah office.

Here she worked, together with her small staff of assistants, invariably accompanied by Emma Ehrlich, for thirty years her private secretary, friend and companion.

Henrietta Szold's right-hand man was Hans Beyth. He had immigrated from Berlin in 1934, and became her assistant in all practical affairs. Together, they met every ship arriving with Youth Aliyah children in Haifa harbor. Together, they worked out the necessary preparations and conducted the new arrivals to their homes. Together, they found solutions to the thousands of problems, which cropped up all the time.

In December 1947, at the outset of the Arab-Jewish war, Hans Beyth went to Haifa, despite the ambushes which were laid every day on the roads, to receive another contingent of Youth Aliyah children and arrange for their accommodation. On the way home, his bus came under Arab sniper fire and he was killed.

On her flower balcony

Henrietta Szold lived in two rooms in a Jerusalem boarding house. The larger room was her office. There, she would begin her working day, in the early days at 5:30 a.m., later on, when a sixteen-hour day no longer sufficed, at 4:30 a.m. Here she wrote letters in her clear small hand, to young people, to friends and family. Here she dictated letters, reports and administrative outlines to her secretary. Here, too, she would receive her fellow-workers in the evening, discussing the problems of the coming days.

She always found time for her flowers and plants. They stood on the window sills and on the floor, on the tops of cupboards and on the balcony.

One of the bookcases held a photograph of her father, whose spiritual heir she always felt herself to be. "My father's daughter *said*", she told me once, "my mother's daughter *did*."

The five parchment-bound volumes of the Hebrew Bible and her prayer books were flanked by Sabbath candlesticks and family photographs. Other shelves contained works of Jewish literature, *The Letters of Gertrude Bell*, Breasted's *History of Egypt*, Richard Llewellyn's *How Green was my Valley*, Sinclair Lewis's *It Can't Happen Here* and other modern novels, as well as Heinrich Graetz's monumental *History of the Jews*, which she had translated into English, and Louis Ginzburg's four-volume *Legends of the Jews*, her labor of love.

Henrietta Szold was expert both in the art of listening and of asking questions. She was interested in anyone sitting opposite her: a politician, a soldier, a child; a young girl in trouble; a youthful delinquent, stubborn and defiant; a helpless outsider, who wanted to break away from a Youth Aliyah group. Her eyes and words penetrated the walls of formal and spiritual convention. Charm, and a great sense of humor accompanied, like a counterpoint, even the most serious conversation. And people trusted her; this above all was the secret of her attraction for all those with whom she spoke.

Her books, her family pictures and her Sabbath candlesticks

In her thousands of letters, Henrietta Szold was fond of writing about her visitors. When the American Presidential candidate Wendell Willkie visited her on his world tour in 1940, as delegate of President Franklin D. Roosevelt, they spoke of the Arab question. "The Jews must have a national homeland," she told him. "I am an ardent Zionist, but I do not believe that there is a necessary antagonism between the hopes of the Jews and the rights of the Arabs."

"It was like a gust of good fresh American air filling my room," she said of this visit. "America will always be a very great country. She produces in her people the greatest assets of humanity: optimism, and a sense of freedom and liberty for yourself as well as for your neighbor."

In reporting this trip in the book *One World*, Wendell Willkie wrote of that hour spent with Henrietta Szold: "As I sat there that late afternoon, with the sun shining through the windows, lighting up that intelligent, sensitive face, I, at least for the moment, wondered if she, in her mature, selfless wisdom, might not know more than all the ambitious politicians."

In her early years in Palestine, before she reached the age of seventy, Henrietta Szold would quite often use a donkey for visiting remote settlements. Later, she used buses or hired a car. The very idea of an official car, only to be used on trips in connection with her position, was anathema, a waste of the public funds entrusted to her. She never set out on her drives to meetings or on tours of inspection any later than seven o'clock in the morning. No sooner had the car got under way, then Hans Beyth would pull out the files. The day's work would be discussed and decided on there and then. Now and again the car would stop, if Miss Szold caught sight of an unusual flower, or to give a lift to young hitchhikers. Once it was a twelve-year old runaway. For the next hour the adventurous boy reduced us all to fits of laughter with his anecdotes and amusing observations. In Jerusalem, he spent the night in the apartment of one of Miss Szold's assistants. He returned to his group next morning in high spirits, proud at having stated his complaints to Miss Szold in person.

Top left: Henrietta Szold discusses with a Youth Aliyah girl the girl's problems
Top right: Wendell Wilkie, U.S. presidential candidate, visits Henrietta Szold
Bottom: With her right-hand man, Hans Beyth, discussing a group's problems

An important object of such trips were the meetings with representatives of settlements offering to take in groups of young people.

The journeys often lasted two or three days. The nights were then spent in Haifa or Tiberias. In Tiberias it was, that supper was interrupted one evening by a telephone call from Jerusalem: Hans Beyth had become the father of a baby girl an hour ago. The occasion was duly celebrated. Later, after Miss Szold had gone to bed, Hans Beyth and I went off to tell the news to some friends, and we continued to celebrate until every bottle in the house was emptied. We returned to our hotel well past midnight, swaying somewhat unsteadily on our feet. At that stage, we were moved to sing a serenade beneath Miss Szold's window. "But pianissimo!" Hans warned. We sang tenderly and softly, or so we thought. A window opened and we heard Miss Szold's voice declaiming in mock operatic tones: "... and ye troubadours do I thank very kindly indeed!"

We were returning to Jerusalem once, after an exhausting day of motoring over appalling roads to six settlements scattered in Galilee and in the Jordan valley. It was a dark night and a heavy rain was beating against the car windows. "We promised to visit the group in Ashdot Ya'aqov this evening! They're expecting us," said Miss Szold.

"I told them on the telephone that we would only be coming, if we could get there before seven," Hans Beyth reassured her.

"That's fine," was the answer. "We can just make it before seven, I'm sure. After all, they're expecting us!" The car turned round and we drove back to Ashdot Ya'aqov. She *was* expected. The group was already sitting round the table in one of the wooden huts.

First she questioned the boys and girls, who had all arrived in the country six months before. How were they getting along in their new surroundings? As was always her way in such conversations, she aired difficulties about which she had been briefed beforehand, and encouraged the young people to talk about these problems. Then she listened intently to every word they had to say. She answered each youngster individually, she analyzed, explained, reported.

* * *

The group had grown restless. For many months, they had received no news from their parents in Europe. Was there nothing they could do?

Several of the boys thought of returning to Europe by clandestine means and trying to rescue their families. Could Miss Szold help them with their plans?

Top: On her tours she meets youngsters
Bottom: Henrietta Szold and Hans Beyth conferring with Kibbutz members

Henrietta Szold told the boys of the efforts made by Jewish organizations to aid those trapped in Europe. She told of single groups who had tried to get through to Palestine. "But *your* task is *here*! I know you want to help your people. You can do this best by following the path you have chosen and that path is, at present, your training here in this country. When the time comes, you will be capable of fulfilling the difficult tasks of the future, whatever these may be. But only then!"

* * *

Not far from Jerusalem, five members of a kibbutz had been killed in an Arab ambush. Shortly afterwards, a new settlement was established near the spot where they had lost their lives. It was named, in their memory, Maaleh Hahamishah, 'The Hill of the Five'.

A Youth Aliyah group has asked permission to join the young settlers after they had completed their preliminary schooling. Henrietta Szold went to inspect the settlement. She never allowed graduates to be sent for training to dangerous points in the country .

An armed guard escorted us all the way up from the road where we had left the car.

Travel had become dangerous in Palestine in the troubled years before the Second World War. Incited by the Grand Mufti of Jerusalem, who was then a secret, and later, an open ally of Hitler, the disturbances of 1936 alone had cost seven hundred Jewish lives, and at times it was possible to travel only with an armed military escort. The Jews threw back more than a thousand attacks on their settlements and institutions.

Henrietta Szold abhorred violence. She never ceased to hope for Arab-Jewish conciliation. She believed this understanding could be achieved.

* * *

The young settlers of Newe Ilan discuss their plans. First, the soil must be cleared of stones. This work will take about two years. But they are already planting a forest. They intend to plant fruit trees here too, plums, peaches and vines. The slopes of the hills would be terraced for this purpose. "And you shall have the first grapes from our vineyards, Miss Szold. We'll bring them over to you in Jerusalem!"

"These bare hills here were orchards once before, in the days of the Biblical Kings," was her reply, "and now you are turning them into orchards again. It will mean hard work - but you will succeed."

She inspects the buildings and admires the extraordinary view stretching across the hills down to the Mediterranean Sea.

< *In the newly founded Kibbutz Ma'ale Hahamishah in the Judean Hills, 1936*

Newe Ilan, 20 Sept. 1941

Dear Father,

It's nearly a year now since you escaped to America, and I've already been here three years. As you will see from my address, I am now in a new place, Newe Ilan. This is how it happened. Our group completed training a year ago. We stayed together for an additional year. Now we are joining the pioneer group here. We'll be living in tents for the next few months, after which we'll get a loan to build wooden houses. The grounds were turned over to us yesterday. The land is granted permanently to each kibbutz in free tenure by the Jewish National Fund, which has bought it from an Arab effendi landowner. In the afternoon, friends came from other settlements to help us with the first plowing.

Last night we rigged up an "Arch of Triumph", as we called it for fun. We stuck a couple of long planks, flanked by green branches, into two tar barrels, filled them with stones and nailed two boards across them to form an archway. We wrote on wrapping paper an inscription taken from the Book of Ezekiel.

We wrote only the first lines, which I translate for you here, (you'll find them in Ezekiel, Chapter 36, Verse 8):

'But you, O mountains of Israel, shall shoot forth your branches, and yield your fruit to my people Israel: for they will soon come home...'

I, too, drove a plow today on the land..."

< *On the first day of the founding of Newe Ilan, the fields are plowed*

Miss Szold shared their midday meal. "Your parents lived in Germany and Austria, in Greece and in Poland, in Yemen and in France", she told them, "but you're going to become something new. Here in this land, we want to become a single nation on our own soil."

* * *

In the morning they had been working in the fields, harvesting olives, tending the farm animals, in the kitchen, in the sewing room, in the flower garden, in the tree nursery, and in the carpentry shop. In the afternoon, they had attended classes in Hebrew, History, The Bible, Botany, Mathematics, Geography.

Now they are sitting together on the stony ground between the oleander bushes. At first they had talked, but then, in the brief half hour of twilight, they had grown silent and pensive.

A boy starts singing, the others join in.

> *"Dear Miss Szold, I **must** write to you! Our two-year training will soon be finished. I am really quite happy with my group. It will be staying on here for another year for further training in agriculture. After that, the plan is to establish a new settlement together. But Yochanan and I don't know what we ought to do. I'm very fond of working with children and would like to train as a nurse. And Yochanan is an artist. He paints so well, and would like to show you the drawings in his album. What he'd like best of all, is to go to an art school in Jerusalem.*
>
> *So I'd like to ask whether we may come to Jerusalem and discuss things with you. Maybe I could attend the nurses' training school in Jerusalem. When may we come and see you?*
>
> *p.s. Our madrich, our instructor, helps me with the Hebrew."*

Henrietta Szold received from ten to twenty letters a day from Youth Aliyah children. Many of these were answered personally, others by her associates. Some eighty-five percent of the youngsters stayed on in the settlements. In cases, where an examination revealed them to be specially gifted, the opportunity was given to study in the city. They were given minimum grants available from the small fund reserved for this purpose.

< *Henrietta Szold with a Youth Aliyah group from Austria*

Learning Hebrew

In 1939, the Second World War started. Shortly before, Britain had broken her pledge to establish Palestine as a "legally protected national home for the Jewish people," seeking, expediently, to secure the goodwill of the Arab countries. Jewish immigration was limited now to a nominal minimum.

The Zionists declared that they would not recognize the restriction of immigration into Palestine, even if this immigration were declared illegal by the British Government. One month after the outbreak of war, the British Government intensified its measures, forbidding all Jewish immigration for six months. Ben Gurion declared, "We will fight in the War as if there were no British, and we will fight the British, as if there were no War."

Caught in the death-trap of Europe, Jews tried every conceivable means of escape. Many sought to reach Palestine by barges and in fishing craft. But most of the boats were intercepted by British naval forces and prevented from reaching Palestine. If they did reach Haifa on these "floating hells", they were deported to the island of Mauritius or to other countries. Yet thousands still succeeded in reaching Palestine.

In wartime, Youth Aliyah became a refuge for four thousand children, because as school children, they did not, at that time, fall under the general restrictions. They were brought to Palestine by Henrietta Szold's assistants, first via England and France, then across Sweden and Holland, Yugoslavia, Italy and Turkey, often after years of struggle to obtain transit visas and transport permits.

There was no longer any question of selection and preparation. Now it was a case of rescue at any cost.

There was the further problem of accommodation, because during the war years, building materials could rarely be obtained for other than military purposes. Many young Jews had enlisted as volunteers in the British Army as long as they were not needed in the country itself. There was a shortage of schoolteachers, educators, instructors.

* * *

On a visit to one of the settlements in the Jezreel Valley, Henrietta Szold discusses arrangements for receiving a group of young refugees. The madricha in charge of the Youth Aliyah group in the kibbutz is sitting next to her.

The journey continues to Massada. This settlement, 240 feet below sea level, lies south of Tiberias on the banks of the Jordan. The mountains of Gilead in Jordan rise behind it.

The settlers still live in tents, and it will be some years before they can start building houses for themselves. But the houses for the Youth Aliyah children have been completed on time. On the left is the little schoolhouse.

Discussion of problems of a newly arrived Youth Aliyah group with their housemother (top) and leaders (bottom). Prof. Judah Magnes often accompanied Henrietta Szold on her inspection tours

Top: While Kibbutz members often still lived in tents, Youth Aliyah groups always moved into specially designed houses. Kibbutz Massada. Bottom: Discussion with the young people

Henrietta Szold celebrated her 80th birthday with a Youth Aliyah group. On her left, Recha Freier and Hans Beyth

Top: Henrietta Szold addresses the group.
Bottom: Discussion with an orthodox group   >

December 1940. A group celebrates the completion of its two-year training in Kibbutz Kiryat Anavim in the Judean mountains near Jerusalem. They all escaped from Austria in 1938. There they were a last generation, here they have become the first generation.

Henrietta Szold has come for the occasion. It was the evening of her 80th birthday. Next to her sit Recha Freier, the initiator of the Youth Aliyah idea, and Hans Beyth.

Henrietta Szold tells of the wave of children expected in the country, if they succeed in escaping from the Germans, if they succeed in surviving the perils of the journey through hostile territory, on board leaky old ships or across guarded frontiers and over snowbound passes.

"We have news that the 'Struma', a boat with enough room for one hundred passengers, is en route from the Balkans with refugees from Rumania and Bulgaria. Seven hundred and fifty people live on this ship under horrid conditions. We hope the Turkish Government will allow them to land, so that they may continue their journey in a manner more suited to human beings. Youth Aliyah will place the few immigration certificates still at its disposal to cover the children on the 'Struma'.

"They will be replacing you here. Work and study awaits them, just as hard work is awaiting you, but also a dignified life in our own land... You will be building up a communal settlement, a *kvutzah* of your own. I want to tell you why this thought pleases me so profoundly. In the *kvutzah*, life is creative. In the *kvutzah*, every act of daily life, every job becomes significant, no matter how lowly: from dish-washing to labour in the vineyards and the discussion of an educational program. In the *kvutzah*, you can live according to your own ideals..."

* * *

The little boat 'Struma' never arrived. Afterwards, it was revealed that it was a fifty-foot boat, built for cattle transport on the Danube. On the way from Constanza to Istanbul it was established that of the eight hundred refugees from Rumania and Bulgaria, one hundred and fifty were children. On arrival in Istanbul, the captain notified the port officials that the ship was not seaworthy. But the Turkish authorities refused permission to land. It remained in the harbor for more than two months, while Jewish organizations in America and Palestine sought feverishly to obtain entry permits from the Palestine government for the eight hundred. The final answer of the British Government was that the refugees "had left their own countries of their own free will, without first obtaining their visas as regulations required". Regretfully, His Majesty's Government was, therefore, unable to grant immigration certificates. Finally, as an act of grace, the British Government "relented," allowing only the hundred and fifty children on board to enter Palestine as wards of Youth Aliyah. This news was telegraphed to Istanbul on 24 February 1942, but a Turkish tugboat had already towed the 'Struma' out to open waters. Some hours later the boat sank. All the passengers, except one, were drowned.

< *In Kibbutz Bet Ha'Arava, Youth Aliyah graduates work at desalting Dead Sea water for watering tomatoes*

Henrietta Szold's favorite tree, a centuries old terebinth

'THE TEHERAN CHILDREN'

Top: Teheran children in a camp near Teheran
Bottom: Arriving at Atlit railway station

In the early summer of 1942 some twenty thousand Poles, civilians and soldiers, were evacuated to Iran from the Russian shore of the Caspian Sea. Among them were 484 Jewish adults and 716 Jewish children. These survivors were transferred to one of the camps near the city of Teheran. As a war correspondent of the British Eighth Army, it was there that I saw them in November of the same year, as I came through Teheran on my way north.

I saw hordes of children, half starved, in rags, recovering in the care of the American Red Cross and of a small group of Jewish workers sent from Palestine. Moshe Sharett's wife led this group. She told me the story of the children, and took me to the camp.

"We were many, many," one of them told us, "when we first set out from Poland. Eight thousand perhaps, maybe ten thousand."

But of this group, the total number of all the stragglers who reached Teheran and later Palestine amounted to one hundred and eight. The others are missing.

The pro-Nazi government of the neighboring state of Iraq refused Jewish refugees permission to travel through their country to Palestine, not even in sealed trains or by air. Negotiations, in which representatives of both the British and the American governments also participated, lasted seven months. But the Iraqis refused. The refugees were, at last, transported south on the Trans-Iran railroad to the Persian Gulf, from there by sea to Karachi, in what is now Pakistan. In Karachi, they boarded a British troopship which, after stopping at another Indian port, brought them across the Indian Ocean and the Red Sea to Suez. A special train took them, at last, to Atlit in Palestine.

Of the 716 children, eleven were less than five years old. 145 were not yet ten, 304 were between ten and fifteen when they arrived in Palestine.

124 of these children had lost both parents since they had started on their journey. 154 children had lost their father, 72 their mother.

They arrived in Atlit on February 18, 1943. Thousands had come to welcome them. Henrietta Szold stood waiting for the children, silent and tense. Beside her were her associates: Emma Ehrlich and Hans Beyth. As the train came into sight, someone began to sing the Jewish National Anthem and the crowd took up the theme:

HATIKVAH
(Anthem of Hope)

Kol od balevav...

As long as deep in the heart,	*Our hope is not yet lost,*
the soul of a Jew yearns,	*the hope of two thousand years,*
and towards the East,	*to be a free people in our land,*
an eye looks to Zion.	*the land of Zion and Jerusalem.*

At Atlit railway station

The train comes in. From left: Hans Beyth, Henrietta Szold and Emma Ehrlich

They hold little flags in their hands. Blue and white - the Jewish colors of hope. Jewish soldiers from Palestine, stationed at Suez as part of a British division, had sewn the flags for the children and given one to each, together with a parcel of food and toys.

Three year earlier, these children, with thousands of others, had started out from Poland with their parents, fleeing before the German troops. They had wandered through many countries. Fleeing, driven and hunted, many of them had been killed, many had died an anonymous death. Many had been made orphans or half-orphans. Their eyes are full of mistrust and hostility.

Innocent, they had come to know death and disease, hunger, lice and human brutality.
They no longer trust anybody.

Their hair has not yet regained its natural beauty, not yet recovered from the baldness which came through no fault of their own. They trust no one. They know men and women to be brutes. They enter a camp for the last time. Doctors, beds and new clothing await them. They file in, carrying their belongings, a blanket over their shoulder.

* * *

The child is seven years old. Ever since it could walk, it has been wandering through hostile lands. From Western Poland to Eastern Poland, thence to Russia and on to Siberia and on to Uzbekistan, and on to the Caspian Sea. From the care of a mother, from the protection of a father, the child wandered into exile in hostile countries. Most friends have died of hunger, of exhaustion and disease. But the child survived and continued to wander. The child's brother, who had taken care of him for a while, was shot while looking for food and stealing potatoes. The child and its friends, according to the report, found the body of the brother, eleven years old, shot through the head, the way a wild animal is shot in the woods. The child wandered on.

From the coast of the Caspian Sea the child was brought to a camp near Teheran. There they had shaven off the girl's lice-infested hair, given her food and a place to sleep. The man from the American Red Cross had given her a blanket for keeps. In India, a British soldier had put a tropical helmet on her shaven head and told her not to give it away.

In the bundle in her right hand, she carries a towel, a pair of socks and the remnants of the family home: two photos of father and mother, a broken doll, a woolen scarf that once belonged to her mother, and a couple of pages from a Hebrew prayer book, which she cannot read. Father had given these to her and told her to keep with her always, until she reached Jews again. This would show that she is Jewish, too.

Now, at last, the child has arrived, and kind people have taken her in their arms, lifting her down from the train. Strangers are friendly and tell her they were expecting her. The child smiles.

The arrival

Their worldly possessions

A child arrives. "They lived in the woods, half-naked, exposed to disease, plagued by vermin, starving – and innocent! Many mothers, themselves being hunted, were forced to abandon their children, anonymously, at the doors of Catholic orphanages as their only apparent chance of surviving the barbarians," Henrietta Szold told us.

Now, after forty months of wandering, the boy arrives in the Land of Israel. He is exhausted. For forty months he has not known the warmth and security of a home, and the word "shelter" he knew only in its most primitive sense. He knows no law, other than the law of hunger. When he had not fought for a scrap of food, he had seldom received any.

They have taken away his lousy rags to bring him new clothing. Now he is sitting, naked under the blanket, waiting. A stranger is bending over him, holding a glass of hot milk to his lips.

The way back to human society will not be easy for him. But it won't be too difficult either, for it is a stranger giving him a glass of milk. He doesn't look up. He just drinks, slowly.

Young Zionists gathered up the remnants of the destitute children, leading them on their long journey. A rabbi joined them and remained with them. This is what Rabbi Hirshberg told Henrietta Szold:

"Jews began to flee from Western Poland to Eastern Poland in September 1939, when the Germans introduced their total war of annihilation against our unarmed Jewish men, women and children. In the summer of 1940, all refugees in Russian-occupied Poland, who refused to become Soviet citizens, were deported to prisons and forced labor camps in Northern Russia and Siberia. Once more, families were torn apart – for the second time within a year.

"In the fall of 1941, after Germany had attacked Russia, all the Poles were released from Russian prisons and camps, for now we were allies of Russia. Non-Jewish Polish citizens were evacuated in an orderly manner by the Polish government-in-exile to England and the Near East, Iran, Palestine and Egypt. Arrangements for us *Jewish* Poles were less satisfactory.

"Only a nominal group of Jewish civilians were included in this evacuation. The majority were left to get out as best they could. In groups and alone, we made our way through Russian Central Asia to Uzbekistan. From there to Tashkent, Samarkand and Bukhara, where we arrived in the summer of 1942, about one year later.

"Of the thousands and thousands of Jewish children who started out on the journey from Poland to Palestine, we hoped that some ten thousand would reach their destination. But only 716 children arrived at Teheran. I was told that about 200 more stragglers are on their way here. What happened to the others, we do not know."

With the Teheran Children came a rabbi who tells Henrietta Szold of the journey

Two boys and their sister refuse to be separated and sent to different places

Henrietta Szold promises, they will not be separated

With the help of a Polish and Yiddish interpreter, Henrietta Szold talked with each of four hundred of the "Teheran children", to find out as much as possible about their origin, their family, their age and their religious background. Hans Beyth questioned the remaining three hundred and sixteen in the same way - depending on their answers the children were assigned to orthodox or liberal communities. A pedagogue, a nurse, and a woman welfare worker were present during the interviews, together with one of Henrietta Szold's assistants, who wrote down all the children's statements.
Three children, two brothers and their sister, have already spent four months in a home. They have received medical care and new clothing.

After a long talk, Henrietta Szold tells the three children that on account of the differences in their ages, they are to join three different groups. But, of course, they will see each other often. The three categorically refuse to be separated. Miss Szold again explains everything, slowly, kindly, carefully. The children answer: "No! We cannot be separated." The girl explains: "You must understand that such a thing is impossible! You see, my little brother has no mother any more and no father. *We are* his mother and father now and have to take care of him. He's only a child! Do you understand?"

Miss Szold understands: "I myself will look after your little brother," she says.
"Oh, no," says the girl. "You have not understood after all. I'm sure you would take care of him. But *I am* his sister, *I* must be his mother now. *I* must look after him. If you take us away from him, he will cry all the time. You wouldn't want that, would you? And I would cry all the time, too."

Henrietta Szold is silent for a few minutes, lost in thought. Then her face brightens again.

"Good" she agrees. "You can all three stay together. You are a very good sister."
The little boy had listened to the conversation without saying a word. Now he speaks up:
"Give me your hand and promise," he says. "Swear that you won't take me away and I will believe you."

Henrietta takes the little boy's hand in her own and promises.

* * *

In the summer of 1944, the first youngsters to have been imprisoned in death camps and survived death marches, arrived in Palestine from Rumania. One of them, a Youth Aliyah boy in Maʻaleh Hahamishah, made sketches of his experiences.

His teacher showed the drawings to Henrietta Szold, who was in the hospital at the time. She asked to see the boy. She questioned him closely. Were the drawings original, made from memory? Were they dream impressions of his imagination? "But I took part in the march myself," he answered. "I left out the worst things."

This boy has become the world famous painter Arikha. He lives in Paris.

בדרך למחנה הכוח

Amongst the Teheran children was Avigdor Arikha, who became a famous artist. The inscription says:
" On the way to the concentration camp" (The Henrietta Szold Estate)

"To eternal rest"

They have been bathed and given fresh clothing, and each child has a bed of its own. Doctors have examined them and they have to take medicines. But they are allowed to sleep as long as they like. Someone comes to talk to them in their own language, alone, during a walk perhaps, and at long last they dare to speak of their parents, and to cry.

After a few weeks, they make their first trip through the country. A little boat takes them up the Jordan, out on Lake Kinneret, which is also called the Sea of Galilee, Sea of Ginnesar and Lake Tiberias. They meet boys and girls not older than themselves, who call out "Shalom!" in passing. "Shalom" is the greeting of the country and means "Peace."

"Peace!" - they are still suspicious of the word. But gradually they feel that they are welcome. Expected. Welcomed. Cared for – all new experiences.

They can even complain if they want to, and people will listen. There is no longer any need to be on guard, to be forever on the lookout. They are no longer in danger. They are no longer fleeing. They are no longer hunted. Occasionally, one or another steals bread, and hides it under a mattress, until it gets moldy.

They roam through the country and meet friends. They climb the hill at Megiddo. There they see the grain stores and stables, belonging once to a cavalry garrison in King Solomon's fortress. They wander through meadows to the Kishon River, where once the prophetess Deborah led the Israelites against the invading Canaanites.

< *In the Valley of Jezreel. In the background – Megiddo*

< < *The first excursion on the Jordan River*

In the village of Bet Yizhaq a new Torah scroll is brought to the synagogue

In Bet Yizhaq, a village near the coast, they encounter a group of young people, escorting a scroll of the Torah, salvaged from a German synagogue and now carried in procession to its new home.

They arrive at a kibbutz and take part in the feast of Passover, commemorating the Exodus from Egypt, from the land of captivity to the land of freedom.

In the afternoon, they see the ceremony of gleaning the first ears of corn. The men who founded the village many years ago, cut the corn, together with their eldest sons. The daughters bind the sheaves. Dressed in their Pesach finery, the girls gather for the traditional dances.

Jews rebuild the land, Jews keep their feasts, Jews defend themselves like other free citizens on free soil -- slowly the nightmare memories of Christian Europe begin to fade.

They sit in the dining hall specially decorated for the occasion, and they take part in the feast celebrating the Exodus from Egypt, when Moses led their forefathers from slavery into freedom. They eat unleavened bread and bitter herbs and sing the songs of the country. The walls are hung with pictures showing the tyranny of old, but also the new life in their own country.

Many settlements asked Henrietta Szold to send them children for the two-year training. But she would only agree to such requests, when she had convinced herself that the conditions of hygiene, the cultural atmosphere and the educational possibilities satisfied her high standards. A separate group of Youth Aliyah houses with dormitories, dining room and classrooms was then built within the community with the aid of loans. Teachers, instructors and house mothers were selected, and a madrich (teacher), chosen for the special qualities and capabilities essential for a leader in charge of the group and familiarity with the children's mother tongue.

"I envy you," Henrietta Szold once addressed a group of such leaders. "Your duty lies defined before you. The darker the outlook, the more clearly you see your task - to teach, to train, to influence, to open up vistas into the past and into the future. It is for you to heal wounds inflicted by malignant cruelty, to replace the ties wrenched away, that bound a generation of children to fathers and mothers, to restore confidence in men and in their works, to evoke powers and direct them to worthy ends, to set up ideals in conformity with the secular achievements of humanity and Jewish endeavor, to strengthen the moral fibre, to encourage aspirations and direct these into channels of action towards culture and peace..."

In Mishmar Ha'emeq, they watch the gleaning of the first corn of the year

Harvest celebration

Youth Aliyah houses in Kibbutz Yagur

<   *They participate in the seder at Kibbutz Mishmar Ha'emeq*

Whenever possible, the Youth Aliyah houses were built on ground belonging to a kibbutz, but some distance away from the houses of the adult settlers. In the Yagur settlement, situated in the bay of Haifa, they lie far from the main road, between trees and gardens, at the foot of Mount Carmel. Each Youth Aliyah group invariably forms a small community of its own within the larger community of the settlement.

Three or four children share a room. The simple furniture comes from the carpenter's shop of the kibbutz. Henrietta Szold's assistants have made sure that the furniture was designed along practical lines, that every child has his or her own shelf, and that the lighting is comfortable. The youngsters

decorate the rooms as they wish, according to their individual taste. The boys and girls are responsible for keeping the rooms tidy and arranging flowers in every room.

They learn to work, and they begin to understand nature. They wait for the first rainfall and watch the clouds pass by. They see the storks fly away to the north and they are concerned for the harvest.

Now that they are on their own soil, the sky above is also theirs.

In the afternoon there are classes. In the orthodox-religious settlements, the boys wear a skullcap, while in other communities their heads are bare. But in all of them, they learn Hebrew and History, Geography and Botany, Mathematics and the Historical Geography of their country.

Not all the children were educated in these self-contained units within communal settlements. Many were housed in agricultural boarding-schools, enlarged by the Youth Aliyah Organization.

One such children's village is Me'ir Shefeya in the mountains of Samaria, where there are between three and four hundred children from Yemen and other eastern countries, brought together with children from North Africa and from the cities of Israel. Here, and in other children's villages and settlements, a favorite project of Henrietta Szold's was realized: to educate children from Israel itself together with new immigrants. In Me'ir Shefeya the children have their own self-government, advised by adult instructors. They are schooled in agriculture, and receive training in trades and handicrafts.

Work in the cowshed

After their first year of training, boys in the locksmith's shop learn to work independently, but under the supervision of an adult mechanic. All the children's shoes are repaired in the shoemaker's workshop. The apprentices spend two or three hours each day working here.

The dairy farm provides milk products for all the inhabitants of the children's village, as well as selling some in town.

Every boy and girl in Youth Aliyah has kitchen duty for a period of two months, and has to clean the washrooms for two months. For two months, they each work in the vegetable and flower gardens; for two months each of the girls works in the sewing room and in the chicken coop. The boys work for two months each in the cowshed or sheep-fold, on reforestation, in the fields, in the workshops, assisting in construction work. A general training in agriculture is thus achieved.

The stone floors of the rooms are mopped every day by the young people. They make their own beds and brush their shoes.

The Youth Aliyah orchestra at Me'ir Shefeya is giving a concert for Miss Szold and her travel companion of the day, Professor Judah Magnes, the President of the Hebrew University of Jerusalem. The two were friends ever since Henrietta Szold's days in New York. They met through Zionist work and made many common efforts in Palestine to bring about more Jewish-Arab understanding.

During a visit to the children's village, the girls perform a Biblical dance for Henrietta Szold. In the foreground dance a Yemenite and a Kurdish girl. They both sewed and embroidered their own festive dresses.

Before and after the evening meal, the children write letters, read, get together to sing or dance, and stroll in the hills.

During their two years with Youth Aliyah, they are trained in all fields of agriculture

Serving each other

Youth Aliyah orchestra in Me'ir Shefeya

With Professor Judah Magnes

Excursion

Folkdance

Top: Discussion of future projects with the heads of Zionist organizations and with the president of Hadassah

With its members, she discusses the building of a new Kibbutz in Galilee, Kfar Szold

For four years a kibbutz, whose members had come from Germany and Hungary in 1933/34, had cultivated a piece of land south of Tel Aviv. They had lived in tents and had cleared the ground - which proved too salty for agriculture. Now, at last, they will be settled permanently in Upper Galilee, close to the Syrian border. They decided to name their kibbutz "Kfar Szold", which means "Szold Village". Henrietta Szold discusses with the kibbutzniks the plans for Youth Aliyah houses to be built in Kfar Szold.

Miss Szold was the trustee of Youth Aliyah as well as of the Hadassah Organization and WIZO, which paid the greatest part of the expenses. The treasurer of the Jewish Agency gave every assistance. At the annual meetings of the board of the Hadassah Organization, she discussed further developments and the budget involved.

During the war years, cloth was scarce in Palestine. Again and again, Henrietta Szold convinced the Moller brothers of the need of cloth for her youngsters. The Moller brothers were the owners of Palestine's only textile factory, the Ata Works in Haifa Bay. "We need cloth for three thousand youngsters, and we need it in four months' time" she said pointedly on this occasion. "We have no choice but to deliver", one of the brothers answered. Henrietta Szold laughed: "And I have no choice but to agree with you gentlemen," she said

On the way to an agricultural school, a hay wagon blocked the narrow country lane. A boy drove the horses, and two others sat on top. "Shalom, boys!", called Hans Beyth, "Where do you come from?" They told him, and a short conversation followed. The three spoke Hebrew. "How long have you been in the country?" Henrietta Szold wanted to know. "Eight months. We were 'Teheran children'." Henrietta Szold breaks the silence, as we drive on: "Eight months in the country... only eight months in the country..."

In the Youth Aliyah houses, Henrietta Szold first looks at the closets and linen cupboards. Then she discusses housekeeping with the housemother.

As always, Henrietta Szold is immediately surrounded by young people and involved in conversation. There aren't only serious problems to be discussed. "When will we be shown a film again?", one boy wants to know, and another asks her to decipher the characters on an old coin that he found while working in the fields. "This is Greek," Miss Szold answers, "One of the many languages I never learned. But perhaps I can send you a Greek textbook. If you're interested in old coins, perhaps why not try to learn the Greek language. Perhaps you will become an expert in it, or an archaeologist - that is a very adventurous profession." Henrietta Szold liked the word "perhaps", she liked to fulfill more than she promised.

Ashdot Ya'aqov, in the Jordan Valley, is one of the oldest and largest settlements in Israel. It owns and works a furniture factory. This formerly swampy area was made arable for large banana plantations.

On her trips, Henrietta Szold liked to make a detour to visit the flower nursery of Ashdot Ya'aqov, where, in addition to native flowers, new varieties from Europe and tropical countries are being cultivated.

Henrietta Szold had many friends in the settlements. The fruit growing expert in 'En Harod shows her a California pear, which he successfully transplanted from America to the Jezreel Valley. Henrietta Szold discovers that the fruit tastes excellent. The two talk about the transplanting of fruits - and of human beings. About active assimilation, which is good, and passive assimilation, which can be bad. They talk about the possibilities of a creative assimilation of children in Israel. Both are optimistic.

Henrietta Szold quotes Colonel T.H. Lawrence's remark, that the Zionists would feel completely at home in Israel after three generations. She believes that it will not take more than two generations, and probably only a single one, if the children come to the country at an early age.

There isn't a single youth group in the country that wasn't visited by Henrietta Szold. She knew hundreds of children by name, she had studied their life history, was familiar with their problems, and followed their development.

<   *Henrietta Szold is greeted by two former "Teheran Boys"*

Inspecting the laundry

On her visits, she talked with every child who had a special request. Before that, however, she talked with the whole group. In these conversations, she always began with the special problems of the individual group in front of her. Today, for instance, the unaccustomed work was the problem under discussion.

"What did you expect things to be in this country before you came here? Are you disappointed? Do you dislike *learning* or do you dislike *working*?... Would you like to hear what I did when I was a child? In the mornings, I worked, like you do here. I picked lint with my sisters, to be made into bandages for the wounded. In the afternoon, I studied and played, just like you do. But then I was younger than you are now.

"There was a war going on in America, where I was born. It was a war for the liberation of Negro slaves, of whom you have heard in school. There was much harm done to many, and there was much injustice done. But in the end, not only were the Negroes made free people again, but another aim was achieved too. The North and the South were united. It was the beginning of the United States of America as we know it today.

"When I was four years old, I helped to pick lint for making bandages. You are older than four. You can help in these times of war and unrest in the world by making something beautiful or something useful in this country. You can, for instance, with your own hands, change a small piece of barren earth in the backyard of your home here into a flowerbed. You have done that already, you say? Well, then you have achieved something, and you probably love this flowerbed the more, because you yourselves have made it blossom. You have worked hard, I take it, but as you like the outcome of your work, you probably like the work itself. This is what I mean. By working and by learning, you are helping in a very great cause - you are helping your Jewish people to rebuild this country. Your flowerbed is yours only because you made it yourselves. Don't forget this!"

Henrietta Szold has talked with the children. She has negotiated with village representatives and discussed agricultural training with them, financial problems - the loan for a new dormitory for forty children expected to arrive soon. Then she had taken a walk through the settlement.

< Powwow

"Can California fruit successfully be transplanted to the soil of Israel?"

<   *In a Kibbutz in the Jordan Valley*

Henrietta Szold hears complaints...

"When I was 4 years old, I helped to pick lint for making bandages..."

"That was 4 years after the war for the liberation of Negro slaves..."

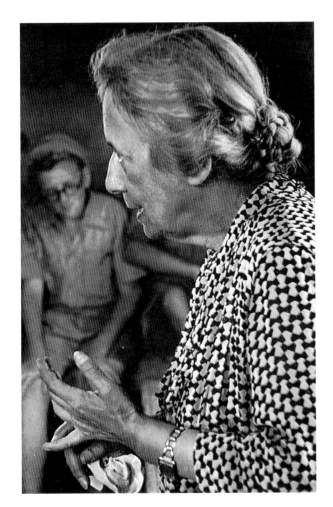

"You are helping your own people to build the country!"

*"We are now free
citizens in our own country..*

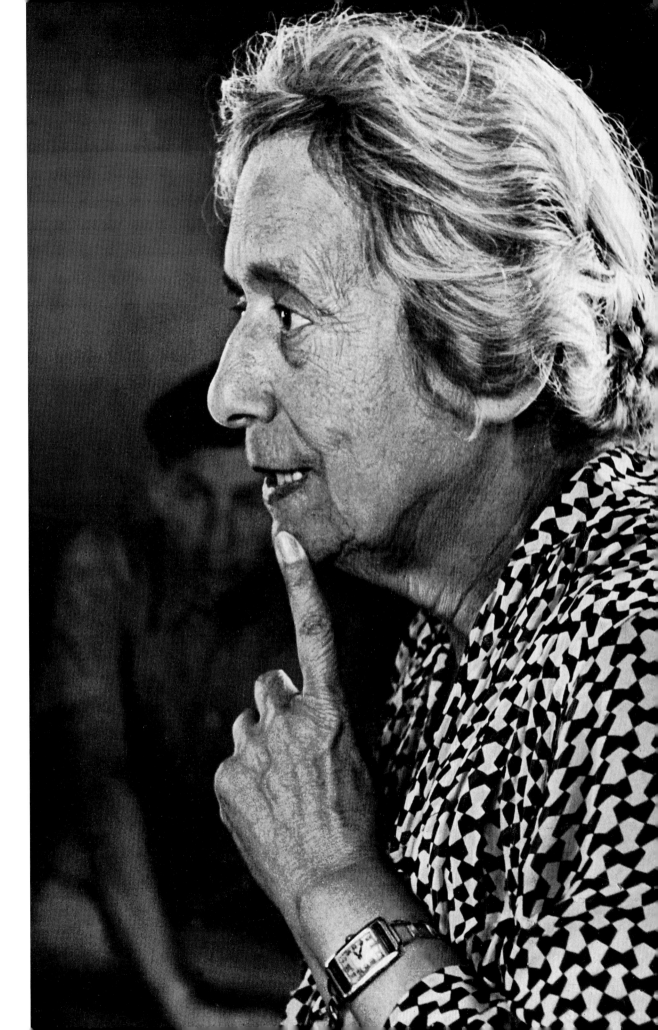

"Please Miss Szold, dance the Horah with us!" ... and she joins the dance

Now she is going back to the car with Hans and Emma. The children have gathered together and surround her, "Please Miss Szold, dance a Horah with us!"

"Oh no, children, thank you really, but I couldn't do that. It is rather late in the day for me to dance a Horah, but I will look on."

"Miss Szold! Dance a Horah with us! Please dance a Horah with us! Please dance with us!"

Henrietta Szold stops. Quietly she laughs to herself. Some thought seems to amuse her deeply, and she joins the dance.

The rose was her favorite flower. Of all fruits, she liked the pear best, and of all vegetables, the cucumber. When Henrietta Szold stayed for lunch, hosts diplomatically prepared the meal accordingly.

In all of Palestine, her favorite tree was an ages-old sycamore near Ramle, on the road from Jerusalem to Haifa.

Whenever the car passed by there, Oscar, the chauffeur, would stop to give Miss Szold time to look at "her" tree and to show the guests travelling with her the old giant with its far-reaching branches. Sometimes Hans Beyth would tease her: "Miss Szold, did you forget your morning exercises today? We must make up for that!" - and with a mighty leap, he jumped aloft and chinned a few times on a branch. Henrietta Szold enjoyed the joke very much, and once she answered: "You know full well that I've never in my life missed my five minutes of morning exercises, and I must warn you: Perhaps I can still chin without breathing as hard as you are doing just now!"

"Herr Dr. Gidal, how old is this tree, do you think?" Henrietta Szold once asked me. She was always formal when she addressed anyone. Hans Beyth was always "Herr Beyth" to her.

* * *

As we leave a village, two auxiliary policemen stop the car. They are Youth Aliyah graduates who want to talk to Miss Szold.

Four hundred Youth Aliyah pupils joined the police in the years up to 1945, and more than fifteen hundred were volunteers in the British Army and the Jewish Brigade of the Eighth Army during World War II.

* * *

Henrietta Szold has given the madrich of the group a lift to the next village, where he wants to discuss the participation of the young people in the orange harvest. But after leaving the car, there is still another short conversation, about a difficult boy.

Her favorite tree. "So old and still bearing fruit"   >

At the entrance to the next village, boys and girls of Youth Aliyah are at work sorting and packing oranges.

During the harvest, the normal course of training is interrupted, and all help where they are needed.

Kibbutz Alonim – the word means 'Oaks' – lies between oak groves on the southwestern spurs of the Galilean mountains. The place was founded after the usual two-year training, and a further one and a half years of pioneer work by that first group, which came to the country from Germany in 1934.

After the first difficult years, with their usual growing pains, Kibbutz Alonim developed so well, that the young settlers were themselves entrusted with the education and training of Youth Aliyah children.

On the stony ground between the oaks, a new tree nursery is being laid out. A few years ago, the instructor was herself a newly-immigrated pupil. Now she is teaching the next generation of children.

Not all the members of Youth Aliyah go with their friends to found new settlements. One boy in the 'Alonim' group, for instance, went to the Bezalel Art School in Jerusalem and became an internationally famous painter. Yet another became district commander in Be'er Sheva'. Youths from other groups became teachers, government officials, officers, scientists. One of Israel's Chiefs of Staff, Lt. Gen. David Eleazar, was a "Teheran child", so was one of Israel's foremost educators, as well as the State Attorney who prosecuted Eichmann.

* * *

On the road to Tel Aviv, eight kilometers from Jerusalem, there stands a Youth Aliyah home. Fifty orphaned orthodox children live here.

Today is an important day. Every Jewish boy, raised in accordance with tradition becomes, on the Sabbath after his thirteenth birthday, a Bar Mitzvah, a "son of obligations". He thus becomes an accountable member of the Jewish community.

Most of the children in this home do not remember their birthday. They forgot it in the years spent in flight. For this reason, seven boys, about thirteen years of age, celebrate their Bar Mitzvah together today.

During the service, each of the boys reads aloud a section from the handwritten parchment scroll, known as the Torah, containing the five Books of Moses. The little brother of one of the boys has pushed his way toward the front.

<   *Two of the first Youth Aliyah boys became auxiliary policemen*

The boys cover themselves with their prayer shawls and face in the direction of Jerusalem, as all pious Jews everywhere in the world do during prayer.

Destoning the ground of Massadah

Kibbutz Matzubah was founded by ninety youngsters. It lies on the wooded hills of northern Israel, close to the Lebanese border. The ground is rocky. Four years after its founding, water still has to be brought from far away. In the fifth year, enough water was found in the village itself at least for drinking and cooking. The winter rain is collected in cisterns.

"Our main work is removing stones from the ground," the settlers inform Henrietta Szold. "Actually, they're not stones but boulders, which we break out of the ground and carry away. In three or four years, we will have cleared all the boulders from the ground. For the time being, we live mainly from this work. We have also been able to lay out a few vegetable patches between the boulders. They are sufficient for our own needs. Only they swallow up all the water from our cisterns. In addition, we are planting trees, olives, plums and carob.

"We have forty goats and a few cows. We still have to buy fodder for the cows. But in our hand-weaving mill we are already making material for our own consumption and for sale. In five or six years we will be well off. We also have eight babies - they're your 'grandchildren', Miss Szold."

"Matzubah", Henrietta Szold wrote "will prove the truth of the old saying: Where there's a will, there's a way. Matzubah was the test case. More than that, it can be cited as justification for the whole Zionist enterprise in Palestine. Difficulties- yes. But..."

Harvesting oranges >

Planting a tree in Alonim

Talented Youth Aliyah graduates are given stipends for further education

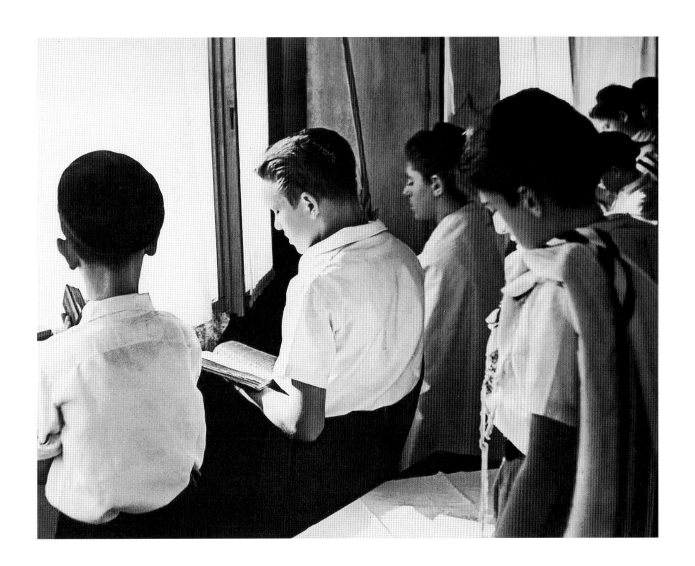

<   *Seven orphan boys, who do not know their exact birthday, celebrate Bar Mitzvah together*

Her first "grandchild"

Intimate conversation

Kfar Szold, a village in Upper Galilee, was founded in 1938. Behind it rise the Syrian highlands and the snow-capped Mount Hermon, where the Jordan has its source. Down in the valley, a chain of new Jewish villages spreads out *on both sides of the river.* To the right, the fields slope up to the Golan Heights, Syrian cannon are visible. The sun breaks through the winter clouds and bathes Kfar Szold in its light.

EPILOGUE

Hadassah Hospital on Mount Scopus, Jerusalem

A procession of mourners, amongst them Professor Chaim Weizmann, Hans Beyth,
Mrs. Weizmann, the Anglican Archbishop of Jerusalem

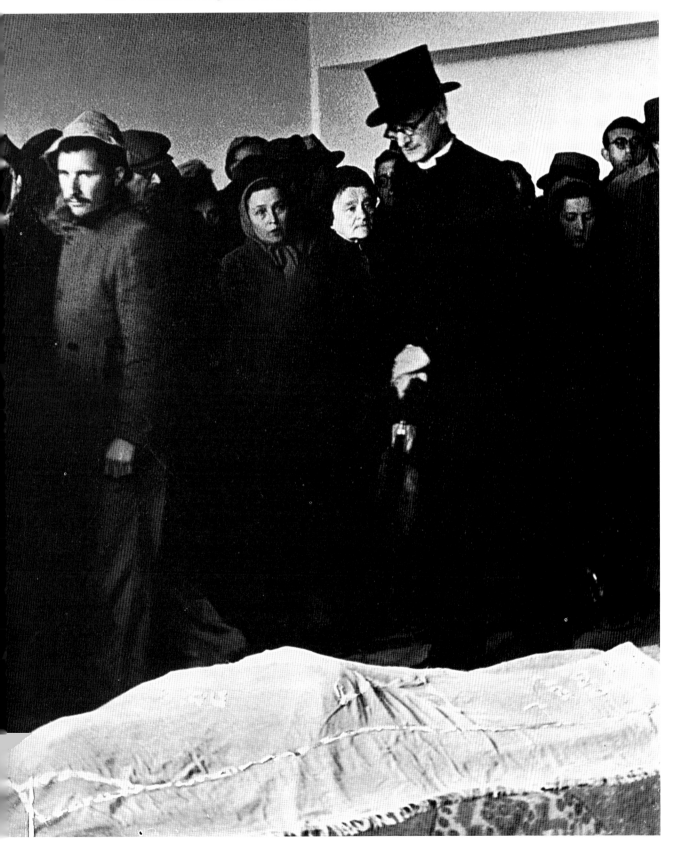

In March 1944, the University of Boston awarded Henrietta Szold the honorary degree of Doctor of Humanities, "as scholar, classicist, journalist; distinguished for social settlement work in America and Palestine; founder of Hadassah; accomplisher of unparalleled reclamation and rehabilitation; Mother in Israel through organizing and directing Youth Aliyah, the joyful mother of ten thousand motherless children." The ceremony was transmitted from America by radio. Henrietta Szold replied from her room in Jerusalem. In a short radio address to those assembled for the ceremony in Boston University, she expressed her "deep appreciation in these days of man's inhumanity to man, to bear the title of Doctor of Humanities."

"It is not a slight honor. You promise me privileges connected with the honor and you warn me of responsibilities. Is it possible to add to the privilege, to represent the thousands of parents whose children have been educated for intelligent democratic citizenship in the homeland of the Jewish renaissance, and the tens of thousands who look for the rescue of their tortured children? As for the responsibilities, I can only divulge that in Zion I have felt the influence of the law of kindness and truth, which demands readiness to shoulder responsibility with forgetfulness of self."

Several days later, Henrietta Szold had to be taken to the hospital. The eighty-three-year-old, who had hardly ever known a respite from work, agreed to go only on condition that she could work there. The hospital room did become a workroom. After a few weeks, she was able to go back home again. Thereafter, she left her room only to be driven the few hundred yards to the office, the doctor having forbidden her to go on foot. Only once did she make an exception.

Some weeks later, Henrietta Szold contracted pneumonia. She was again taken to the Hadassah Hospital on Mount Scopus, and later to the adjacent Nurses Training Home, which she had founded many years before. She died there on February 13, 1945, at the age of eighty-four.

Henrietta Szold's mortal remains lie in a hall of the Hadassah Nursing School, on a wooden bier, "close to the ground," as prescribed by Jewish tradition. She is covered with a curtain of the sacred Torah ark, and eight candles are lit at her head. Thousands have come. Professor Weizmann and his wife stand before her.

An endless line of children passes by to pay their last respects to the woman who saved their lives and their souls, when they had almost been lost.

Henrietta Szold once complained: "I should have had children, many children." When she died, she left behind thirteen thousand mourning children.

A seemingly endless funeral procession follows the coffin from Mount Scopus to the Mount of Olives. On the left, back of the grounds of the Hebrew University, the land drops to the Desert of Judea.

It is a cold day. A biting wind blows from the east over the crest of the Mount of Olives.

Below, behind medieval walls, rises the city of Jerusalem, and the Dome of the Rock stands out clearly against the stone pavement of the Temple Square. For a few seconds, the sun breaks through the heavy layer of clouds and then disappears again.

A rainbow arches across the sky, and Jerusalem glows in the afternoon sun.
The mourners hurry to the open grave of Henrietta Szold.
In accordance with her wishes, no obituary speeches were made when she was buried.
A child from Youth Aliyah recited the prayer that is said at the open grave of a mother.

* * *

Seven days after Henrietta Szold's death, Professor Judah Magnes delivered the memorial address at the funeral solemnities.

"If you wish to know what is meant by the ethics of Judaism, search within the conscience of Henrietta Szold. If you wish to gain insight into the Jewish conscience, listen to her voice - a voice inspired by the lightning of Sinai and the Prophets of Israel and by the still, small voice of the traditionally compassionate woman in Israel, who, throughout the generations, hearkens to the weeping of mothers and children.

"That thin, frail frame was the embodiment of Jewish morality. Every word that passed her lips was carefully weighed and had its source in an innate purity - even the words spoken in the asperity of argument and the pleasantries of her lighter moods. The motive of her every act was honest and pure, completely without thought of self.

"In her parents' home she learned to hold fast to the ancient bonds of Jewish ethical and religious tradition, a tradition containing the often opposing qualities of justice and mercy. Only those endowed with a divine gift have the power of carrying out both precepts together.

"Along with her austere obedience to the dictates of the moral law, what delicacy of feeling, what nobility were hers and how great the compassion that enveloped her entire being like a mantle of holiness.

"In all the annals of mankind I know of no greater, more sacred devotion, and in this integrity of purpose she walked all her life.

"Without aspiration to greatness, she was great.

"She aspired to the sources of true life, and her own life would have been impossible and meaningless without her belief in eternity, in the God of Israel. She tried, with might and main, with body and soul, to walk humbly with her God."

The funeral procession stretches from Hadassah Hospital on Mount Scopus to the Mount of Olives

Kaddish is recited by a Youth Aliyah boy

The grave

"Illegal immigrants" on their night journey to a Kibbutz where some of the younger ones will join Youth Aliyah groups

The Second World War was over. The concentration camps and death houses of Europe were opened. The truth was more dreadful than the most horrible rumors had given reason to believe. Only five of every hundred Jews in Europe were still alive.

They wanted to go home, to the Land of Israel.

There were close to 200,000 who set out.

The British Government under Prime Minister Clement Attlee and Foreign Secretary Ernest Bevin refused to allow them to enter. The quota was to be 2,000 immigrants per month. Not one Jew above this number was to set foot in their land of hope.

The Jews answered with guerilla war against British military camps, against the British administration, against the British apparatus built up to prevent Jewish immigration. At the same time, mass immigration into Palestine was organized. Delegates were sent to Europe. Whole groups were smuggled across many frontiers, often with the help of the governments of the countries, to secret collecting points on the Mediterranean coast. The transports, led by members of Jewish intelligence organizations, had to travel by night in order to evade the network of British observers.

The fully packed ships then departed and tried to slip through the blockade maintained by the British navy in the Mediterranean.

In two years the Haganah, the defense organization of the Jews of Palestine, brought more than 100,000 "illegal persons" into the country. Many Haganah ships were captured by British warships and ordered to return to Europe. All refused to do so, after which they were escorted to Haifa. The refugees were forcibly removed from the ships, and deported in British ships to the island of Cyprus. The number of persons interned there finally totalled 24,000. The Haganah ship "Exodus 1947," with space for 800 passengers, began its voyage from the coast of France with 4,554 home-comers. It was discovered by the British navy in the Mediterranean. After a stubborn battle, in which three Jews were killed, it was rammed, and surrendered. The ship was brought to Haifa and from there, with a British crew, taken back to Germany together with its passengers. This time, on personal orders from Foreign Secretary Bevin, even the children were deported again.

This incident did its share in turning world opinion more and more against the anti-Jewish Palestine policy of the British Government. Many British soldiers and officers in Palestine, disgusted at their Government's policy, sympathized openly with the Jews, and some helped them actively.

In the late fall of 1947, the United Nations decided on the suspension of Great Britain's mandate over Palestine and on the establishment of two independent states in its place, Jewish and Arab. The first two countries to recognize the Jewish State in Palestine were the United States of America and the Soviet Union.

The "Exodus", built for 800 passengers, with 4,554 refugees, limps into Haifa harbour after being captured by the British navy

A girl comes to Palestine on a Haganah ship. Like all the others, she is taken off the ship in the harbor of Haifa and searched for weapons. The soldiers check her belongings. She produces all that has been left to her from the countries of western civilization: a piece of cloth, a comb, photographs of her dead mother.

Then she is taken aboard a deportation ship to internment in Cyprus.

They came from Buchenwald...

In the last weeks before liberation, the older boys had hidden the youngest in a large rubbish box during the day, because he would otherwise have been destroyed as being too young for work.

After several months in a recreation camp, the survivors were able to travel, and sailed to Palestine; they were permitted to land, because they came under the quota of 2,000 allowed to enter the country each month. The youngest carries the flag. He is now Chief Rabbi Israel Meir Lau. Far left: his older brother, Naftali Lavi.

The youngest boy, Israel Meir Lau, carries the flag.   >
He is now Chief Rabbi of Israel

On May 14, 1948, the independent State of Israel was proclaimed by David Ben Gurion

The British mandate over Palestine had been declared at an end by the General Assembly of the United Nations.

On 14 May, 1948, in a ceremony at the Tel Aviv Museum, the independent State of Israel was proclaimed.

Professor Chaim Weizmann became the first President of the new State, David Ben Gurion its Prime Minister and Minister of Defense.

The armies of five Arab states, the Arab Legion under its British commander, Brigadier Glubb, attacked the new state from all sides. After a long and bloody struggle, they were defeated and driven out of the Land of Israel.

T h e   g a t e s   o f   I s r a e l   o p e n e d .

Survivors

First, the 24,000 internees from Cyprus were brought home, 3,000 Youth Aliyah children were among them.

Then the flood of immigration began, from Europe, Egypt, North Africa, from India, Yemen, Iraq, Iran, The Soviet Union and Ethiopia.

The Jewish population of the country rose from 600,000 at the beginning of the year 1948, to over 2 million in the year 1962 and to over 5 million in 1996.

In December 1960, the 100,000th Youth Aliyah child came with other immigrants by air from Iran to Israel. Both the pilot of the plane and the stewardess had once been brought to the country through Youth Aliyah.

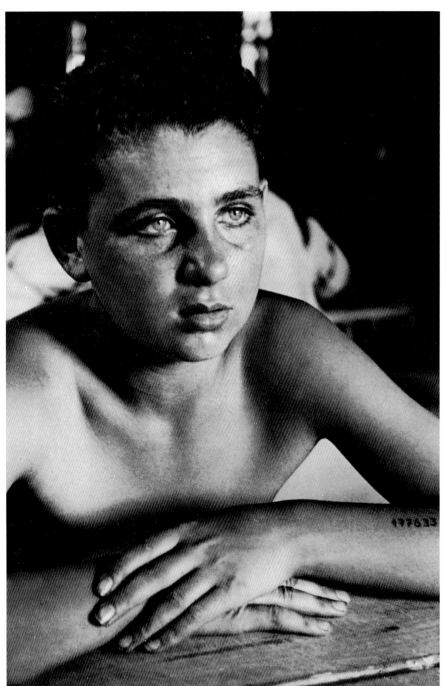

From Dachau...

From Mauthausen...

... but they also came from Sweden and England, where they had fled during the war. They came from Italy and Holland, where some people had granted them asylum or had hidden them.

They came from Bulgaria and Denmark, whose kings had protected them. They declared that their people would wear the Yellow Star with the Jews, but that they wouldn't deliver a single Jew to the Germans.

In Denmark, many had been saved by a German, S.F. Duckwitz, who warned them and thus made possible their flight to Sweden in time.

They came from Yugoslavia and Hungary, from Rumania and Poland, from Turkey, from Iran and Iraq, from Tunis and from Egypt, from Russia and from Ethiopia.

They came
from Yemen...

They came
from Algiers...

They came
from Libya...   >

They came from Morocco...   *They came from Ethiopia...*

More than 300,000 Jews came from the countries of North Africa alone. Like all other immigrants, they lived for years in tents or barracks, until they found work and living quarters in the newly-built settlements and in the cities.

A host of problems was the result of the mass immigration of these years; above all, health problems, educational problems, social problems.

These were precisely the problems to which Henrietta Szold had dedicated her life. She had laid some of the foundation stones of the future State of Israel. Then came the crowning achievement of her life: the rescue of the children.